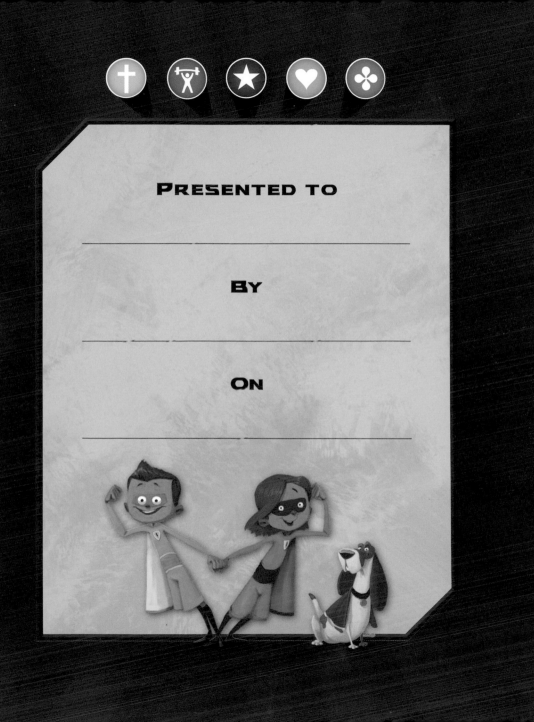

PRESENTED TO

_____

BY

_____

ON

_____

ZONDERKIDZ

Super Heroes Storybook Bible
Features Copyright © 2018 by Jean E. Syswerda
Illustrations © 2018 Josh O'Brien

This title is also available as a Zondervan ebook.

Requests for information should be addressed to:

Zonderkidz, 3900 *Sparks Dr. SE, Grand Rapids, Michigan 49546*

ISBN 978-0-310-75018-5

Art direction and design: Jody Langley

Printed in China

18 19 20 21 22 23 /DBS/ 22 21 20 19 18 17 16 15 14 13 12 11 10 9 8 7 6 5 4 3 2 1

SUPER HEROES
STORYBOOK BIBLE

ILLUSTRATED BY **JOSH O'BRIEN**

FEATURES WRITTEN BY **JEAN E. SYSWERDA**

Z | ZONDERkidz

SUPER HEROES
TABLE OF CONTENTS

SUPER HERO DECODER

✝	Believes	✓	Obeys
B	Brave	P	Patient
☼	Cheerful	⚡	Self-Controlled
⟳	Faithful	🏋	Strong
F	Forgiving	🗣	Tells Others
G	Giving	❀	Thankful
★	Helpful	T	Tries Hard
H	Honest	◆	Trusted
K	Kind	W	Wise
♥	Loving		

Ultimate Super Hero

OLD TESTAMENT

The Lord and King gives me strength.

He makes my feet like the feet of a deer.

He helps me walk on the highest places.

—Habakkuk 3:19

NOAH AND THE FLOOD

Genesis 6–9

Noah was a godly man. He was without blame among the people of his time. He walked faithfully with God.

God saw how sinful the earth had become. All its people were living very sinful lives. So God said to Noah, "Make yourself an ark out of cypress wood. I am going to bring a flood on the earth. Everything on earth will die. But I will make my covenant with you.

You will go into the ark. Your sons and your wife and your sons' wives will enter it with you. Bring a male and a female of every living thing into the ark. Two of every kind of bird, animal, and every kind of creature that moves along the ground. All of them will be kept alive with you."

Noah did everything just as God commanded him.

Rain fell on the earth for 40 days and 40 nights. The waters rose on the earth until all the high mountains under the entire sky were covered. Everything on earth was destroyed. Only Noah and those with him in the ark were left.

The waters flooded the earth for 150 days. But God showed concern for Noah. God sent a wind to sweep over the earth. And the waters began to go down.

After 40 days Noah opened a window he had made in the ark. Then Noah sent out a dove. But the dove couldn't find any place to rest. Water still covered the whole surface of the earth. So the dove returned to Noah in the ark. He waited seven more days. Then he sent out the dove again. In the evening the dove returned to him. There in its beak was a freshly picked olive leaf! So Noah knew that the water on the earth had gone down.

Then God said to Noah, "Come out of the ark. Bring the birds, the animals, and all the creatures that move along the ground. They can have little ones and the number of them can increase." So Noah came out of the ark.

Then God blessed Noah and his sons. He said, "I am now making my covenant with you and with all your children who will be born after you. I am making it also with every living creature that was with you in the ark. The waters of a flood will never again destroy the earth."

God continued, "Here is the sign of the covenant I am making. I have put my rainbow in the clouds. It will be the sign of the covenant between me and you and every kind of living creature."

SUPER ME

Obeying God isn't always easy. Sometimes what he wants you to do is hard. But it's worth it. Noah and his family were blessed because he obeyed God. And you will be too!

POWER SURGE

OBEYS ✓

"Noah did everything just as God commanded him."
—Genesis 6:22

ABRAHAM TRUSTS IN GOD

Genesis 18; 21

The LORD appeared to Abraham near the large trees of Mamre. Abraham was sitting at the entrance to his tent. Abraham looked up and saw three men standing nearby. So he quickly left to greet them. He bowed low to the ground.

He said, "My LORD, if you are pleased with me, don't pass me by. Let me get you something to eat to give you strength. Then you can go on your way."

So Abraham hurried into the tent to Sarah. "Quick!" he said. "Get about 36 pounds of the finest flour. Prepare it and bake some bread."

Then he ran over to the herd. He picked out a choice, tender calf. He gave it to a servant, who hurried to prepare it. Then he brought some butter and milk and the calf that had been prepared. He served them to the three men. While they ate, he stood near them under a tree.

"Where is your wife Sarah?" they asked him.

"Over there in the tent," he said.

Then one of them said, "I will surely return to you about this time next year. Your wife Sarah will have a son."

Sarah was listening at the entrance to the tent. Abraham and Sarah were already very old. Sarah was too old to have a baby. So she laughed to herself. She thought, "I'm worn out, and my husband is old. Can I really know the joy of having a baby?"

Then the Lord said to Abraham, "Why did Sarah laugh? Why did she say, 'Will I really have a baby, now that I am old?' Is anything too hard for me? I will return to you at the appointed time next year. Sarah will have a son."

The LORD was gracious to Sarah, just as he had said he would be. The LORD did for Sarah what he had promised to do. Sarah became pregnant. Abraham was 100 years old when his son Isaac was born to him.

Sarah said, "God has given laughter to me."

SUPER ME

Even when you are sad or bad things happen, even when you feel alone, God is there, and you can trust him.

POWER SURGE

BELIEVES ✝

"[Abraham] believed the LORD. The LORD was pleased with [Abraham] because he believed. So [Abraham's] faith made him right with the LORD."

—Genesis 15:6

JOSEPH AND HIS BROTHERS

Genesis 37; 39; 41–42; 45

F

JOSEPH

Joseph was a young man. Israel loved Joseph more than any of his other sons. Israel made him a beautiful robe. Joseph's brothers saw that their father loved him more than any of them. So they hated Joseph. They couldn't even speak one kind word to him.

Joseph had a dream. When he told it to his brothers, they hated him even more. He said to them, "Listen to the dream I had. We were tying up bundles of grain out in the field. Suddenly my bundle stood up straight. Your bundles gathered around my bundle and bowed down to it."

His brothers said to him, "Do you plan to be king over us? Will you really rule over us?" They didn't like what he had said.

Joseph's brothers had gone to take care of their father's flocks. Joseph went to look for them. But they saw him a long way off. Before he reached them, they made plans to kill him.

"Here comes that dreamer!" they said to one another. "Let's throw him into one of these empty wells. Let's say that a wild animal ate him up. Then we'll see whether his dreams will come true."

When Joseph came to his brothers, they threw him into the well. As they did, they saw some Ishmaelite traders coming from Gilead.

Judah said, "Let's sell him to these traders." Judah's brothers agreed with him. They sold him to the Ishmaelite traders for eight ounces of silver. Then the traders took him to Egypt.

An Egyptian named Potiphar had bought him from the Ishmaelite traders who had taken him there. Potiphar was one of Pharaoh's officials.

When two full years had passed, Pharaoh had a dream. In the morning he was worried. So he sent for all the magicians and wise men of Egypt. Pharaoh told them his dreams. But no one could tell him what they meant. So Pharaoh sent for Joseph.

Pharaoh told Joseph what he had dreamed. Then Joseph said to Pharaoh, "God has shown Pharaoh what he's about to do. Seven years with plenty of food are coming to the whole land of Egypt. But seven years when there won't be enough food will follow."

Pharaoh said to Joseph, "I'm putting you in charge of the whole land of Egypt." Joseph was 30 years old when he began serving Pharaoh, the king of Egypt. During the seven years there was plenty of food. Joseph collected all the extra food produced in those seven years in Egypt. He stored it in the cities.

The seven years when there was plenty of food in Egypt came to an end. Then the seven years when there wasn't enough food began. It happened just as Joseph had said it would.

Ten of Joseph's brothers went down to Egypt to buy grain there. Joseph was governor of the land. When Joseph's brothers arrived, they bowed down to him. Joseph recognized his brothers, but they didn't recognize him.

Joseph said to his brothers, "I am Joseph! Is my father still alive?" But his brothers weren't able to answer. They were too afraid of him.

Joseph said, "I am your brother Joseph. I'm the one you sold into Egypt. But don't be upset. And don't be angry with yourselves because you sold me here. God sent me ahead of you to save many lives."

Joseph kissed all his brothers and wept over them.

SUPER ME

Joseph knew that God had brought good out of the bad that happened to him. You can forgive like Joseph. It will take God's help. But you can forgive those who hurt you.

POWER SURGE

FORGIVING **F**

"Forgive your brothers. Forgive the terrible things they did to you. Forgive them for treating you so badly."

—Genesis 50:17

BABY MOSES

Exodus 1–2

The people of Israel had many children. There were so many of them that they filled the land.

Then a new king came to power in Egypt. Joseph didn't mean anything to him. "Look," he said to his people. "The Israelites are far too many for us. We must deal with them carefully."

Pharaoh gave an order to all his people. He said, "You must throw every Hebrew baby boy into the Nile River."

A man and a woman from the tribe of Levi got married. [Jochebed] became pregnant and had a son. She hid him for three months. After that, she couldn't hide him any longer. She got a basket made out of the stems of tall grass. She coated the basket with tar. She placed the child in the basket. Then she put it in the tall grass that grew along the bank of the Nile River. The child's sister wasn't very far away. She wanted to see what would happen to him.

JOCHEBED

Pharaoh's daughter went down to the Nile River to take a bath. She saw the basket in the tall grass. When she opened it, Pharaoh's daughter saw the baby. He was crying. She felt sorry for him. "This is one of the Hebrew babies," she said.

Then his sister spoke to Pharaoh's daughter. She asked, "Do you want me to go and get one of the Hebrew women? She could breast-feed the baby for you."

"Yes. Go," she answered. So the girl went and got the baby's mother. Pharaoh's daughter said to her, "Take this baby and feed him for me. I'll pay you." So the woman took the baby and fed him. When the child grew older, she took him to Pharaoh's daughter. And he became her son. She named him Moses. She said, "I pulled him out of the water."

SUPER ME

Are you brave? Or mostly scared? Jochebed was definitely afraid. But she knew she had to save her son. When something frightens you, remember Jochebed.

POWER SURGE

BRAVE B

"She saw that her baby was a fine child. And she hid him for three months."
—Exodus 2:2

MOSES LEADS HIS PEOPLE

Exodus 3; 7; 13; 14, 21–28

Moses was taking care of the flock of his father-in-law. Moses led the flock to the western side of the desert. He came to the mountain of God. There the angel of the LORD appeared to him from inside a burning bush. Moses saw that the bush was on fire. But it didn't burn up.

God spoke to him from inside the bush. He called out, "Moses! Moses!"

"Here I am," Moses said.

"I am the God of your father. I am the God of Abraham. I have seen how my people are suffering in Egypt. So I have come down to save them from the Egyptians. I will bring them into a good land. So now, go. I am sending you to Pharaoh. I want you to bring the Israelites out of Egypt."

Moses spoke to God. "Who am I that I should go to Pharaoh?" he said. "Who am I that I should bring the Israelites out of Egypt?"

God said, "I will be with you. I will give you a sign. It will prove that I have sent you. When you have brought the people out of Egypt, all of you will worship me on this mountain."

Then the LORD said to Moses, "I have made you like God to Pharaoh. And your brother Aaron will be like a prophet to you. You must say everything I command you to say. I will use my powerful hand against Egypt. When I judge them with mighty acts, I will bring my people Israel out like an army on the march."

Pharaoh let the people go. God led the people toward the Red Sea by taking them on a road through the desert.

The Egyptians went after the Israelites. All Pharaoh's horses and chariots and horsemen and troops chased them. The Israelites were terrified. They cried out to the LORD. They said to Moses, "What have you done to us by bringing us out of Egypt?" Moses said, "Don't be afraid. You will see how the LORD will save you today."

Moses reached out his hand over the Red Sea. The LORD pushed the sea back with a strong east wind. He turned the sea into dry land. The waters were divided. The people of Israel went through the sea on dry ground.

The Egyptians chased them. All Pharaoh's horses and chariots and horsemen followed them into the sea. At sunrise the sea went back to its place. The Egyptians tried to run away from the sea. But the LORD swept them into it. The water flowed back and covered the chariots and horsemen. It covered the entire army that had followed the people of Israel into the sea.

SUPER ME

Some people are strong because of their huge muscles. Some people are strong because they are smart. But the best way to be strong is to rely on God's strength instead of your own. Next time you think you just can't do something, ask God for his help.

POWER SURGE

STRONG 🏋️

"The LORD spoke to Moses. He said, 'When you return to Egypt, do all the amazing things I have given you the power to do.'"
—Exodus 4:21

MIRIAM GIVES THANKS

Exodus 14–15

MIRIAM

The LORD saved Israel from the power of Egypt. The Israelites saw the amazing power the LORD showed against the Egyptians. So the Israelites had great respect for the LORD and put their trust in him.

Aaron's sister Miriam was a prophet. She took a tambourine in her hand. All the women followed her. They played tambourines and danced. Miriam sang to them.

"Sing to the LORD. He is greatly honore

"He has thrown Pharaoh's horses and chariot drivers into the Red Sea."

SUPER ME

You can praise God in many ways. If you can't dance, sing. If you can't sing, play an instrument. If you can't play, just speak your words of praise. God is just as worthy of your praise today as when he saved the Israelites. So, be a Miriam and praise God!

RAHAB AND THE SPIES

Joshua 1–2; 6

The LORD spoke to Joshua. Joshua was Moses' helper. The LORD said "I want you and all these people to get ready to go across the Jordan River. I want all of you to go into the land I am about to give to the Israelites. Be strong and brave. Do not be afraid. I am the LORD your God. I will be with you everywhere you go."

So Joshua gave orders to the officers of the people. He said, "Go through the camp. Tell the people, 'Get your supplies ready. Three days from now you will go across the Jordan River right here. You will go in and take over the land. The LORD your God is giving it to you as your very own.'"

RAHAB

Joshua sent two spies. He said to them, "Go and look over the land. Most of all, check out Jericho." So they went to Jericho. They stayed at the house of Rahab.

The king of Jericho sent a message to Rahab. It said, "Bring out the men who came into your house."

But the woman had hidden the two men. She had taken them up on the roof. The king's men left to hunt down the spies.

Rahab went up on the roof before the spies settled down for the night. She said to them, "I know that the LORD has given you this land. We are very much afraid of you. The LORD your God is the God who rules in heaven above and on the earth below.

"Now then, please give me your word. Promise me in the name of the LORD that you will be kind to my family. Promise that you won't put any of us to death."

So the men made a promise to her. "If you save our lives, we'll save yours," they said.

The gates of Jericho were shut tight and guarded closely because of the Israelites. No one went out. No one came in.

The LORD said to Joshua, "I have handed Jericho over to you. March around the city once with all your fighting men. In fact, do it for six days. On the seventh day, march around the city seven times. The wall of the city will fall down."

On the seventh day, they got up at sunrise. They marched around the city. The priests blew the trumpets. As soon as the army heard the sound, they gave a loud shout. Then the wall fell down. Everyone charged straight in.

The young men who had checked out the land went into Rahab's house. They brought her out along with her parents and brothers and sisters. They brought out everyone else there with her. They put them in a place outside the camp of Israel.

SUPER ME

Rahab believed God and bravely did what she knew was right. You can be like her! Bravery is something God will give you if you believe in him. He'll help you do what you know is right.

POWER SURGE

BRAVE (B)

"Here is what I am commanding you to do. Do not be afraid. Do not lose hope. I am the LORD your God. I will be with you everywhere you go."

—Joshua 1:9

DEBORAH LEADS AN ARMY

Judges 4–5

Deborah was a prophet. She was leading Israel at that time. Deborah served the people as their judge.

Deborah sent for Barak. Deborah said to Barak, "The LORD, the God of Israel, is giving you a command. He says, 'Go! Take 10,000 men. Lead them up to Mount Tabor. I will lead Sisera into a trap. He is the commander of Jabin's army. I will bring him, his chariots and his troops to the Kishon River. There I will hand him over to you.'"

Barak said to her, "If you go with me, I'll go. But if you don't go with me, I won't go."

"All right," Deborah said. "I'll go with you. The LORD will hand Sisera over to a woman."

Sisera gathered together his 900 chariots. He also gathered together all his men. He brought them to the Kishon River.

Then Deborah said to Barak, "Go! Today the LORD will hand Sisera over to you." So Barak went down Mount Tabor. His 10,000 men followed him.

B

DEBORAH

As Barak's men marched out, the LORD drove Sisera away from the field of battle. The LORD scattered all of Sisera's chariots. Barak's men struck down Sisera's army with their swords.

On that day Deborah and Barak sang a song.

"The princes in Israel lead the way. The people follow them just because they want to. When this happens, praise the LORD!

"Kings, hear t

I will pr

So the land was at peace for 40 years.

When Deborah was leading her people as a judge or in battle, most other women were at home cooking and taking care of children. But Deborah obeyed God and followed his call. Do you ever think you're different from the other kids around you? So was Deborah. God will use your special gifts to do good things for him—maybe even win battles!

POWER SURGE

HELPFUL ★

"Those who lived in the villages of Israel would not fight. They held back until I, Deborah, came. I came as a mother in Israel."

—Judges 5:7

...rs, listen! I will sing to the LORD.

...LORD in song. He is the God of Israel."

THE MIGHTY WARRIOR

Judges 6–7

The Israelites did what was evil in the sight of the LORD. So for seven years he handed them over to the people of Midian. The Midianites treated the Israelites very badly.

The angel of the LORD appeared to Gideon. He said, "Mighty warrior, the LORD is with you."

"Pardon me, sir," Gideon replied, "you say the LORD is with us. Then why has all this happened to us?"

The LORD turned to Gideon. He said to him. "You are strong. Go and save Israel from the power of Midian. I am sending you."

"Pardon me, sir," Gideon replied, "but how can I possibly save Israel? My family group is the weakest in the tribe of Manasseh. And I'm the least important member of my family."

The LORD answered, "I will be with you. So you will strike down the Midianites."

So Gideon blew a trumpet to send for the men of Abiezer. He told them to follow him. He called for the men of Manasseh to fight. He also sent messengers to the men of Asher, Zebulun and Naphtali. So all those men went up to join the others.

The Lord said to Gideon, "I want to hand Midian over to you. But you have too many men for me to do that. Tell them, 'Those who tremble with fear can turn back.'" So 22,000 men left. But 10,000 remained.

The Lord said to Gideon, "There are still too many men. With the help of 300 men I will save you. Let the other men go home."

So Gideon sent those Israelites home. But he kept the 300 men. They took over the supplies and trumpets the others had left.

Gideon separated the 300 men into three fighting groups. He put a trumpet and an empty jar into the hands of each man. And he put a torch inside each jar.

"Watch me," he told them. "Blow your trumpets from your positions all around the camp. And shout the battle cry, 'For the LORD and for Gideon!'"

When the 300 trumpets were blown, the LORD caused all the men in the enemy camp to start fighting one another. The army ran away. Gideon and his 300 men were very tired. But they kept on chasing their enemies. Gideon chased them and captured them. He destroyed their whole army.

SUPER ME

Gideon and his little army did big things for God. He can use you just like he used Gideon. Maybe you won't conquer an enemy army, but you can win small battles for God. Make someone in your family happy, help someone at school, or be kind to a stranger.

POWER SURGE

STRONG

"The angel of the LORD appeared to Gideon. He said, 'Mighty warrior, the LORD is with you … You are strong. Go and save Israel from the power of Midian. I am sending you.'"

—Judges 6:12, 14

RUTH AND NAOMI

Ruth 1–4

† B T RUTH

Naomi's husband died. So she was left with her two sons. They married women from Moab. One was named Orpah. The other was named Ruth. Naomi's family lived in Moab for about ten years. Then Mahlon and Kilion also died. So Naomi was left without her two sons and her husband.

While Naomi was in Moab, she heard that the Lord had helped his people. He had begun to provide food for them again. So Naomi and her two daughters-in-law prepared to go from Moab back to her home.

Naomi said to her two daughters-in-law, "Both of you go back. Each of you go to your own mother's home. You were kind to your husbands, who have died. You have also been kind to me. May the Lord be just as kind to you."

Orpah kissed her mother-in-law goodbye. But Ruth held on to her. "Don't try to make me leave you and go back. Where you go I'll go. Where you stay I'll stay. Your people will be my people. Your God will be my God." Naomi realized that Ruth had made up her mind to go with her. So the two women continued on their way.

They arrived in Bethlehem just when people were beginning to harvest the barley. Ruth said, "Let me go out to the fields. I'll pick up the grain that has been left behind."

Naomi said to her, "My daughter, go ahead." So Ruth went out to a field and began to pick up grain. As it turned out, she was working in a field that belonged to Boaz. He was from the family of Elimelek.

Boaz said to Ruth, "Dear woman, listen to me. Don't pick up grain in any other field. Don't go anywhere else. Stay here."

When Ruth heard that, she bowed down with her face to the ground. She asked him, "Why are you being so kind to me? I'm from another country."

Boaz replied, "I've been told all about you. I've heard about everything you have done for your mother-in-law since your husband died. I know that you left your mother and father. I know that you left your country. May the LORD reward you for what you have done."

"Sir, I hope you will continue to be kind to me," Ruth said. "You have made me feel safe."

Boaz married Ruth. The LORD blessed her so that she became pregnant. And she had a son. They named him Obed. He was the father of Jesse. Jesse was the father of David.

Most people today don't worship idols made of wood or stone. Perhaps their idol is money or music. Whatever gets between you and God is an idol. Ruth never looked back at the idols she worshipped as a child. She knew she had met the one true God, and she followed only him.

POWER SURGE

BELIEVES ✝

"Ruth replied, 'Don't try to make me leave you and go back. Where you go I'll go. Where you stay I'll stay. Your people will be my people. Your God will be my God.'"

–Ruth 1:16

HANNAH'S PRAYERS ARE ANSWERED

1 Samuel 1

Hannah was very sad. She wept and wept. She prayed to the LORD. She made a promise to him. She said, "LORD, you rule over all. Please see how I'm suffering! Show concern for me! Don't forget about me! Please give me a son! If you do, then he will serve the LORD all the days of his life."

As Hannah kept on praying, Eli watched her lips. She was praying in her heart. Her lips were moving. But she wasn't making a sound. Eli thought she was drunk. He said to her, "How long are you going to stay drunk? Stop drinking your wine."

"That's not true, sir," Hannah replied. I was telling the LORD all my troubles. I've been praying here because I'm very sad."

Eli answered, "Go in peace. May the God of Israel give you what you have asked him for."

HANNAH

63

So after some time, Hannah became pregnant. She had a baby boy. She said, "I asked the Lord for him." So she named him Samuel.

When the boy didn't need her to breast-feed him anymore, Hannah brought the boy to Eli. Hannah said to Eli, "Pardon me, sir. I'm the woman who stood here beside you praying to the Lord. And that's just as sure as you are alive. I prayed for this child. The Lord has given me what I asked him for. So now I'm giving him to the Lord. As long as he lives he'll be given to the Lord."

SUPER ME

Promises aren't always easy to keep. Hannah's promise to God was very hard for her to keep. But she did it. She knew her promise was important. She knew God wanted her to keep it. After all, God had kept his promise to her. God wants you to keep your promises too. Even when it's hard.

POWER SURGE

THANKFUL ♣

"Hannah prayed. She said, 'The LORD has filled my heart with joy. He has made me strong.'"

−1 Samuel 2:1

65

DAVID AND GOLIATH

1 Samuel 17

Saul and the army of Israel gathered together. They lined up their men to fight against the Philistines.

A mighty hero named Goliath came out of the Philistine camp. He was more than nine feet tall. He had a bronze helmet on his head. He wore bronze armor that weighed 125 pounds. He carried a bronze javelin on his back. His spear was as big as a weaver's rod.

Goliath stood there and shouted to the soldiers of Israel. He said, "Choose one of your men. Have him come down and face me. If he's able to fight and kill me, we'll become your slaves. But if I win and kill him, you will become our slaves and serve us."

Saul and the whole army of Israel heard what the Philistine said. They were terrified.

DAVID

David was the son of Jesse, who belonged to the tribe of Ephraim. Jesse's three oldest sons had followed Saul into battle. But David went to Bethlehem to take care of his father's sheep.

Early in the morning David left his father's flock in the care of a shepherd. He ran to the battle lines and asked his brothers how they were.

As David was talking with them, Goliath stepped forward from his line. He again dared someone to fight him, and David heard it.

David said to Saul, "Don't let anyone lose hope because of that Philistine. I'll go out and fight him."

Saul replied, "You are too young. He's been a warrior ever since he was a boy."

But David said to Saul, "I've been taking care of my father's sheep. Sometimes a lion or a bear would come and carry off a sheep from the flock. The LORD saved me from the paw of the lion. He saved me from the paw of the bear. And he'll save me from the powerful hand of this Philistine too."

Saul said to David, "Go. And may the LORD be with you."

David picked up his wooden staff. He went down to a stream and chose five smooth stones. He put them in the pocket of his shepherd's bag. Then he took his sling in his hand and approached Goliath.

Goliath looked David over. He saw how young he was. He said to David, "Why are you coming at me with sticks? Do you think I'm only a dog?"

David said to Goliath, "You are coming to fight against me with a sword, a spear and a javelin. But I'm coming against you in the name of the LORD who rules over all."

As the Philistine moved closer to attack him, David ran quickly to the battle line to meet him. He took out a stone. He put it in his sling. He slung it at Goliath. The stone hit him on the forehead. He fell to the ground. The Philistines saw that their hero was dead. So they turned around and ran away.

David won the fight against Goliath with a sling and a stone. He struck down the Philistine and killed him. He did it without even using a sword.

SUPER ME

David was a brave young man. He wasn't brave because he was strong or smart. He was brave because he knew God was with him. That's where your courage comes from too. Trust God to help you. He'll always be with you.

POWER SURGE

STRONG

"David said to Goliath, 'You are coming to fight against me with a sword, a spear and a javelin. But I'm coming against you in the name of the LORD who rules over all.'"

—1 Samuel 17:45

JONATHAN AND DAVID

1 Samuel 14, 17, 18

JONATHAN

After David killed Goliath, he returned to the camp. From that time on, Saul kept David with him.

Saul's sons were Jonathan, Ishvi and Malki-Shua. Jonathan and David became close friends. Jonathan loved David just as he loved himself. Jonathan made a covenant with David because he loved him just as he loved himself. Jonathan took off the robe he was wearing and gave it to David. He also gave him his military clothes. He even gave him his sword, his bow and his belt.

David did everything Saul sent him to do. He did it so well that Saul gave him a high rank in the army. David led the troops in battle. In everything he did, he was very successful. That's because the LORD was with him. When Saul saw how successful David was, he became afraid of him.

Saul told his son Jonathan and all the attendants to kill David. But Jonathan liked David very much. So Jonathan warned him, "My father is looking for a chance to kill you. Be very careful."

Jonathan told his father good things about David. He said to him "Please don't do anything to harm David. He hasn't done anything to harm you. He put his own life in danger when he killed Goliath. The LORD used him to win a great battle for the whole nation of Israel."

But an evil spirit sent by the LORD came on Saul. He was sitting in his house and holding his spear while David was playing the harp. Saul tried to pin him to the wall with his spear. But David escaped.

David ran to Jonathan. "What have I done? Why is he trying to kill me?"

Jonathan said to David, "I promise that I'll find out what my father is planning to do. Go to the place where you hid when this trouble began." So David hid in the field.

When the time for the New Moon feast came, the king sat down to eat. He spoke to his son Jonathan, "Why hasn't the son of Jesse come to the meal?" Jonathan replied, "David begged me to let him go to Bethlehem."

Saul became very angry with Jonathan. He said to him, "You are an evil son. You have refused to obey me. Send someone to bring the son of Jesse to me. He must die!" Jonathan got up from the table. He was very sad that his father was treating David so badly.

The next morning Jonathan went out to the field to meet David. David bowed down in front of Jonathan. Then they kissed each other and cried. Jonathan said, "Go in peace. In the name of the LORD we've promised to be friends."

SUPER ME

Good friends always want what's best for each other. That's what made Jonathan such a good friend to David. Are you a Jonathan? Do you love anyone more than you love yourself? What would you be willing to give up for your friends?

POWER SURGE

HELPFUL ⭐

"Jonathan said to David, "I'll do anything you want me to do for you."
—1 Samuel 20:4

ABIGAIL SHOWS KINDNESS

1 Samuel 25

B
W
K

ABIGAIL

A certain man in Maon was very wealthy. His name was Nabal. His wife's name was Abigail. She was a wise and beautiful woman. But her husband was rude and mean in the way he treated others.

David was staying in the Desert of Paran. He sent for ten young men. He said to them, "Go up to Nabal at Carmel.

Greet him for me. Say to him, 'May you live a long time! May everything
go well with you and your family! When your shepherds were with us, we
treated them well. Please be kind to my men. Please give me and my men
anything you can find for us.'"

When David's men arrived, they gave Nabal the message from David.
Nabal answered, "Who is this David? Why should I give away my bread and
water? Why should I give food to men who come from who knows where?"

So David's men turned around and went back. They reported to David every word Nabal had spoken. David said to his men, "Each of you put on your swords!" So they did. David put his sword on too. About 400 men went up with David.

One of the servants warned Abigail, Nabal's wife. He said, "David sent some messengers from the desert to give his greetings to our master. But Nabal shouted at them and was rude. Horrible trouble will soon come to our master and his whole family."

Abigail didn't waste any time. She got 200 loaves of bread and two bottles of wine. She got five sheep that were ready to be cooked. She got a bushel of grain. She got 100 raisin cakes. And she got 200 cakes of pressed figs. She loaded all of it on the backs of donkeys.

Abigail rode her donkey into a mountain valley. There she saw David and his men.

When Abigail saw David, she quickly got off her donkey. She bowed down in front of David with her face toward the ground. She fell at his feet. She said, "Pardon your servant, sir. Please don't pay any attention to that evil man Nabal. I've brought a gift for you. Give it to the men who follow you."

David said to Abigail, "Give praise to the LORD. He has sent you today to find me. You have kept me from killing Nabal and his men this day."

About ten days later, the LORD struck Nabal down. And he died. David heard that Nabal was dead. Then David sent a message to Abigail. He asked her to become his wife. Abigail quickly got on a donkey and went with David's messengers. She became David's wife.

SUPER ME

When someone did something wrong—even when that someone was her husband—Abigail stepped in and did the right thing. Sometimes doing the right thing is hard. Sometimes it's scary. Abigail knew all of that. But she still did it. So can you. Next time you have to do something hard, remember Abigail.

POWER SURGE

KIND **K**

"The LORD rewards everyone for doing what is right."
—1 Samuel 26:23

SOLOMON ASKS GOD FOR WISDOM

1 Kings 1–7

SOLOMON

King Solomon went to the city of Gibeon to offer sacrifices. The LORD appeared to Solomon. He spoke to him in a dream during the night. God said, "Ask for anything you want me to give you."

Solomon answered, "You have been very kind to my father David, your servant. That's because he was faithful to you. LORD my God, you have now made me king. I don't know how to carry out my duties. So give me a heart that understands. Then I can rule over your people. I can tell the difference between what is right and what is wrong."

The LORD was pleased that Solomon had asked for that. So God said to him, "You have not asked to live for a long time. You have not asked to be wealthy. You have not even asked to have your enemies killed. Instead, you have asked for wisdom. You want to do what is right and fair when you judge people. Because that is what you have asked for, I will give it to you. I will give you a wise and understanding heart. And that is not all. I will give you wealth and honor. As long as you live no other king will be as great as you are."

So King Solomon ruled over the whole nation of Israel. God made Solomon very wise. His understanding couldn't even be measured. It was like the sand on the seashore. People can't measure that either. Solomon became famous in all the nations around him. The kings of all the world's nations heard about how wise Solomon was. So they sent their people to listen to him.

SUPER ME

What is most important to you? Do you wish you were smarter? Do you wish you had more toys? Next time you pray and ask God for something, remind yourself of what's most important. Not how smart you are. Not how many things you have. But the fact that God loves you and you love him.

POWER SURGE

WISE **W**

"The LORD made Solomon wise, just as he had promised him."
—1 Kings 5:12

ESTHER SAVES HER PEOPLE

Esther 2–8

B
W
K

ESTHER

There was a Jew from the tribe of Benjamin. His name was Mordecai. Mordecai had a cousin named Esther. Mordecai adopted her as his own daughter.

Everyone who saw Esther was pleased with her. King Xerxes like Esther more than any of the other women. So he put a royal crown on her head. He made her queen.

King Xerxes gave Haman a seat of honor. It was higher than the positions any of the other nobles had. All the royal officials at the palace gate got down on their knees. But Mordecai refused to get down on his knees. He wouldn't give Haman any honor at all.

Haman was very angry. He found out who Mordecai's people were. He didn't want to kill only Mordecai. He also looked for a way to destroy all Mordecai's people. They were Jews. He wanted to kill all of them.

Haman said to King Xerxes, "Certain people are scattered among the nations. Their practices are different from the practices of other people. They don't obey your laws. If it pleases you, give the order to destroy them."

The king said to Haman. "Do what you want to with those people."

Mordecai found out about everything that had been done. Then he went out into the city. He wept out loud. He cried bitter tears.

Esther's attendants came to her. They told her about Mordecai. So she became very troubled. Esther sent for Hathak. He was one of the king's officials. She ordered him to find out what was troubling Mordecai.

Hathak went to see Mordecai. He told him everything that had happened to him. He also gave Hathak a copy of the order. It commanded people to wipe out the Jews. Mordecai told Hathak to show the order to Esther. Mordecai wanted her to make an appeal to the king for her people.

Hathak went back and reported to Esther. Then Esther directed him to give an answer to Mordecai. She told him to say, "There is a certain law that applies to any man or woman who approaches the king without being sent for. It says they must be put to death."

Mordecai sent back an answer. He said, "It's possible that you became queen for a time just like this."

Esther sent a reply to Mordecai. She said, "I'll go to the king. I'll do it even though it's against the law. And if I have to die, I'll die." Esther put on her royal robes. The king was sitting on his royal throne in the hall. He saw Queen Esther standing in the courtyard.

The king asked, "What is it, Queen Esther? What do you want? I'll give it to you."

Esther replied, "King Xerxes, if it pleases you, come to a feast today. I've prepared it for you. Please have Haman come with you."

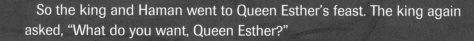

So the king and Haman went to Queen Esther's feast. The king again asked, "What do you want, Queen Esther?"

Then Queen Esther answered, "Your Majesty, I hope you will be pleased to let me live. Please spare my people. My people and I have been sold to be killed and wiped out."

King Xerxes asked Queen Esther, "Who is the man who has dared to do such a thing? And where is he?"

Esther said, "He's this evil Haman!"

Haman was terrified in front of the king and queen. The king got up. He was very angry. The king said to his men, "Put Haman to death!"

That same day King Xerxes gave Queen Esther everything Haman had owned.

The Jews were filled with joy and happiness. They were very glad because now they were being honored.

SUPER ME

Lots of things in life are scary to do. Be an Esther. Don't give up because you're scared. Take a deep breath, say a prayer, and go forward to do what must be done.

POWER SURGE

BRAVE Ⓑ

"I'll go to the king. I'll do it even though it's against the law. And if I have to die, I'll die.'"

—Esther 4:15–16

FOREVER FAITHFUL

Job 1:1—2:10

There was a man who lived in the land of Uz. His name was Job. He was honest. He did what was right. He had respect for God and avoided evil. Job was the most important man among all the people in the east.

One day angels came to the Lord. Satan also came with them. The Lord said to Satan, "Where have you come from?"

Satan answered, "From traveling all around the earth. I've been going from one end of it to the other."

Then the Lord said to Satan, "Have you thought about my servant Job? There isn't anyone on earth like him. He is honest. He does what is right. He has respect for God and avoids evil."

"You always give Job everything he needs," Satan replied. "That's why he has respect for you. Reach out your hand and strike down everything he has. Then I'm sure he will speak evil things against you."

The Lord said to Satan, "All right. I am handing everything he has over to you. But do not touch the man himself."

Then Satan left the Lord and went on his way.

One day a messenger
came to Job. He said,
"The Sabeans attacked
us and carried off the
animals. They killed
some of the servants
with their swords. I'm
the only one who has
escaped to tell you!"

While he was still speaking, a second messenger came. He said,
"God sent lightning from the sky. It struck the sheep and killed them. It
burned up some of the servants. I'm the only one who has escaped to
tell you!"

While he was still speaking, a third messenger came. He said, "The Chaldeans separated themselves into three groups. They attacked your camels and carried them off. They killed the rest of the servants with their swords. I'm the only one who has escaped to tell you!"

While he was still speaking, a fourth messenger came. He said, "Your sons and daughters were at their oldest brother's house. Suddenly a strong wind blew in from the desert. It struck the four corners of the house. The house fell down on your children. Now all of them are dead. I'm the only one who has escaped to tell you!"

After Job heard all these reports, he got up and tore his robe. He shaved his head. Then he fell to the ground and worshiped the LORD. He said,

"The LORD has given, and the LORD has taken away.
May the name of the LORD be praised."

In spite of everything, Job didn't sin by blaming God for doing anything wrong.

His wife said to him, "Are you still continuing to be faithful to the LORD? Speak evil things against him and die!"

Job replied, "We accept good things from God. So we should also accept trouble when he sends it."

SUPER ME

Job was a good man. But terrible things happened to him. That's hard to understand. Today terrible things still happen to people who love God. But you can still choose to follow God and love him, like Job, even when bad things happen.

POWER SURGE

FAITHFUL ⟲

"We accept good things from God. So we should also accept trouble when he sends it." In spite of everything, Job didn't say anything that was sinful.

—Job 2:10

THE VOICE OF THE LORD

Isaiah 6:1–8

I saw the LORD. He was seated on his throne. His long robe filled the temple. He was highly honored. Above him were seraphs. Each of them had six wings. With two wings they covered their faces. With two wings they covered their feet. And with two wings they were flying. They were calling out to one another. They were saying,

"Holy, holy, holy is the LORD who rules over all.
The whole earth is full of his glory."

The sound of their voices caused the stone doorframe to shake. The temple was filled with smoke.

"How terrible it is for me!" I cried out. "I'm about to be destroyed! My mouth speaks sinful words. And I live among people who speak sinful words. Now I have seen the King with my own eyes. He is the LORD who rules over all."

A seraph flew over to me. He was holding a hot coal. He had used tongs to take it from the altar. He touched my mouth with the coal. He said, "This has touched your lips. Your guilt has been taken away. Your sin has been paid for."

Then I heard the voice of the LORD. He said, "Who will I send? Who will go for us?"

I said, "Here I am. Send me!"

SUPER ME

Are you willing for God to use you? Are you too scared? Isaiah was scared. But God wanted him to be his messenger. God wants to use you too. Maybe he wants you to help a friend who is sad. Or to help your mom when she is tired. No matter how sinful—or scared—you are, God can use you, just like he used Isaiah.

POWER SURGE

TELLS OTHERS

"I said, 'Here I am. Send me!' So [the LORD] said, 'Go and speak to these people.'"

–Isaiah 6:8-9

THE FIERY FURNACE

Daniel 2:49; 3

King Nebuchadnezzar appointed Shadrach, Meshach and Abednego to help Daniel govern Babylon and the towns around it.

King Nebuchadnezzar made a gold statue. It was 90 feet tall and 9 feet wide. He set it up near the city of Babylon. Then the king sent for the royal rulers, high officials, and governors. He sent for advisers, treasurers, judges and court officers. He asked them to a special gathering to honor the statue.

Then a messenger called out loudly, "Listen, you people who come from every nation! Here is what the king commands you to do. You must fall down and worship the gold statue. If you don't, you will be thrown into a blazing furnace."

Some people said, "You have appointed some Jews to help Daniel govern. Their names are Shadrach, Meshach and Abednego. They refuse to worship the gold statue you have set up."

Nebuchadnezzar was very angry. He sent for Shadrach, Meshach and Abednego. The king said to them, "Don't you serve my gods? Don't you worship the gold statue I set up? If you won't, you will be thrown at once into a blazing furnace. Then what god will be able to save you from my power?"

Shadrach, Meshach and Abednego replied to him. They said, "We might be thrown into the blazing furnace. But the God we serve is able to bring us out of it alive. He will save us from your power."

Nebuchadnezzar was very angry. He ordered that the furnace be heated seven times hotter than usual. He gave a command to tie up Shadrach, Meshach and Abednego. Then they were thrown into the furnace.

King Nebuchadnezzar leaped to his feet. "Didn't we tie up three men? Didn't we throw three men into the fire?"

They replied, "Yes, we did, Your Majesty."

The king said, "Look! I see four men walking around in the fire. They aren't tied up. And the fire hasn't even harmed them. The fourth man looks like a son of the gods."

The king approached the opening of the blazing furnace. He shouted, "Shadrach, Meshach and Abednego, come out! You who serve the Most High God, come here!"

So they came out of the fire. Not one hair on their heads was burned. They didn't even smell like smoke.

Then Nebuchadnezzar said, "May the God of Shadrach, Meshach and Abednego be praised! He has sent his angel and saved his servants."

SUPER ME

These men knew how important it was to follow God and obey him, no matter what. Even when obeying God meant disobeying the king—even when obeying God meant they would probably die—they obeyed God anyway.

POWER SURGE

BRAVE **B**

"We want you to know this, Your Majesty. Even if we knew that our God wouldn't save us, we still wouldn't serve your gods. We wouldn't worship the gold statue you set up."

—Daniel 3:18

DANIEL AND THE LIONS' DEN

Daniel 6

B
DANIEL
H

It pleased Darius to appoint 120 royal rulers over his entire kingdom. He placed three leaders over them. One of the leaders was Daniel. Daniel did a better job than the other two leaders or any of the royal rulers. So the king planned to put him in charge of the whole kingdom. But the other two leaders and the royal rulers heard about it. So they looked for a reason to bring charges against Daniel. They tried to find something wrong with the way he ran the government. But they weren't able to.

So the two leaders and the royal rulers went as a group to the king. They said, "All the royal leaders, high officials, royal rulers, advisers and governors want to make a suggestion. We've agreed that you should give an order. Here is the command you should make your people obey for the next 30 days. Don't let any of your people pray to any god or human being except to you. If they do, throw them into the lions' den." So King Darius put the order in writing.

Daniel found out that the king had signed the order. In spite of that, he did just as he had always done before. He went to his room three times a day to pray. Some of the other royal officials saw him praying and asking God for help. So they went to the king. They said, "Your Majesty, Daniel still prays to his God three times a day." When the king heard this, he was very upset.

So the king gave the order. Daniel was brought out and thrown
into the lions' den. The king said to him, "You always serve your God
faithfully. So may he save you!"

A stone was brought and placed over the opening of the den.

As soon as the sun began to rise, the king got up. He hurried to the
lions' den. He called out, "Daniel! You serve the living God. You always
serve him faithfully. So has he been able to save you from the lions?"

SUPER ME

Daniel knew it was dangerous to disobey the king's law. But he knew that following God was more important than anything else. Daniel was a person just like you are. God gave him courage to do the right thing. God will give you courage when you choose to do the right thing too.

Daniel answered, "My God sent his angel. And his angel shut the mouths of the lions. They haven't hurt me at all, Your Majesty."

The king was filled with joy. He ordered his servants to lift Daniel out of the den. So they did. They didn't see any wounds on him. That's because he had trusted in his God.

King Darius wrote to people of all nations. He said, "I order people in every part of my kingdom to respect and honor God. He is the living God. He sets people free and saves them. He does miraculous signs and wonders. He does them in the heavens and on the earth."

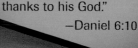

POWER SURGE

FAITHFUL ↻

"Daniel found out that the king had signed the order. In spite of that, he did just as he had always done before ... He got down on his knees and gave thanks to his God."

—Daniel 6:10

SAMSON'S STRENGTH

Judges 15-16

Samson led Israel for 20 years. In those days the Philistines were in the land. One day Samson fell in love. The woman was Delilah. The rulers of the Philistines went to her. They said, "See if you can get him to tell you the secret of why he's so strong. Each of us will give you 28 pounds of silver."

So Delilah said to Samson, "Tell me the secret of why you are so strong. Tell me how you can be tied up and controlled." Samson said, "Let someone tie me tightly with new ropes. Then I'll become as weak as any other man." So Delilah got some new ropes. She tied him up with them. She called out, "Samson! The Philistines are attacking you!" But he snapped the ropes off his arms. They fell off just as if they were threads.

SAMSON

Delilah spoke to Samson again. "You have been telling me lies. This time really tell me how you can be tied up." He replied, "Weave the seven braids of my hair into the cloth on a loom. If you do, I'll become as weak as any other man." So while Samson was sleeping, Delilah took hold of the seven braids of his hair. She wove them into the cloth on a loom. Again she called out to him, "Samson! The Philistines are attacking you!" He woke up from his sleep. He pulled up the loom.

She continued to pester him day after day until he was sick and tired of it. So he told her everything. He said, "My hair has never been cut. If you shave my head, I won't be strong anymore. I'll become as weak as any other man."

Delilah got Samson to go to sleep on her lap. Then she called for someone to cut off his hair. And he wasn't strong anymore.

Then the Philistines grabbed him. They poked his eyes out. They put chains around him.

The rulers of the Philistines were going to celebrate. They said, "Our god has handed our enemy Samson over to us." They shouted, "Bring Samson out. Let him put on a show for us." So they had him stand near the temple pillars. About 3,000 men and women were watching Samson. Then he prayed to the LORD.

"Please make me strong just one more time." Samson reached toward the two pillars that were in the middle of the temple. Then he pushed with all his might. The temple came down on the rulers. It fell on all the people in it. So Samson killed many more Philistines when he died than he did while he lived.

SUPER ME

Don't ever forget that Samson's real strength wasn't in his muscles. It was in God. He forgot that. But you don't have to. No matter what size your muscles—you are someone special and strong in God.

POWER SURGE

STRONG

The woman had a baby boy. She named him Samson. As he grew up, the LORD blessed him. The Spirit of the LORD began to work in his life.

Judges 13:24–25

NEW TESTAMENT

Let the LORD make you strong. Depend
on his mighty power. Put on all of God's
armor … So remain strong in the faith. Put
the belt of truth around your waist. Put the
armor of godliness on your chest. Wear
on your feet what will prepare you to tell
the good news of peace. Also, pick up the
shield of faith. With it you can put out all
the flaming arrows of the evil one. Put on
the helmet of salvation. And take the sword
of the Holy Spirit. The sword is God's word.

–Ephesians 6:10–17

AN ANGEL VISITS MARY

Luke 1:26–38

God sent the angel Gabriel to Nazareth, a town in Galilee. He was sent to a virgin. The girl was engaged to a man named Joseph. He came from the family line of David. The virgin's name was Mary.

The angel greeted her and said, "The Lord has blessed you in a special way. He is with you."

Mary was very upset because of his words. She wondered what kind of greeting this could be.

But the angel said to her, "Do not be afraid, Mary. God is very pleased with you. You will become pregnant and give birth to a son. You must call him Jesus. He will be great and will be called the Son of the Most High God."

"How can this happen?" Mary asked the angel.

The angel answered, "The Holy Spirit will come to you. The power of the Most High God will cover you. So the holy one that is born will be called the Son of God."

"I serve the Lord," Mary answered. "May it happen to me just as you said it would."

SUPER ME

Mary was scared and confused by the angel's message. But that didn't matter to her. What mattered was doing what God wanted. Be a Mary! When you know God wants you to do something—just do it!

POWER SURGE

BELIEVES ✟

"You are a woman God has blessed. You have believed that the Lord would keep his promises to you!"

—Luke 1:45

JOSEPH'S DREAM

Matthew 1:18–25, Isaiah 7:14

JOSEPH

This is how the birth of Jesus the Messiah came about. His mother Mary and Joseph had promised to get married. But before they started to live together, it became clear that she was going to have a baby. She became pregnant by the power of the Holy Spirit. Her husband Joseph was faithful to the law. But he did not want to put her to shame in public. So he planned to divorce her quietly.

But as Joseph was thinking about this, an angel of the Lord appeared to him in a dream. The angel said, "Joseph, son of David, don't be afraid to take Mary home as your wife. The baby inside her is from the Holy Spirit. She is going to have a son. You must give him the name Jesus. That's because he will save his people from their sins."

All this took place to bring about what the Lord had said would happen. He had said through the prophet, "The virgin is going to have a baby. She will give birth to a son. And he will be called Immanuel." The name Immanuel means "God with us."

Joseph woke up. He did what the angel of the Lord commanded him to do. He took Mary home as his wife.

SUPER ME

Be a Joseph. Remember to be kind. Even when others are unkind, even when others don't understand, even when it's hard, be a kind person like Joseph.

POWER SURGE

LOVING ♥

"Joseph woke up. He did what the angel of the Lord commanded him to do. He took Mary home as his wife."
—Matthew 1:24

JESUS IS BORN

Luke 2

Caesar Augustus made a law. It required that a list be made of everyone in the whole Roman world. Everyone went to their own town to be listed.

So Joseph went to Bethlehem, the town of David. Joseph went there with Mary to be listed. Mary was engaged to him. She was expecting a baby.

While Joseph and Mary were there, the time came for the child to be born. She gave birth to her first baby. It was a boy. She wrapped him in large strips of cloth. Then she placed him in a manger.

There were shepherds living out in the fields nearby. An angel of the Lord appeared to them. And the glory of the Lord shone around them. The angel said to them, "Do not be afraid. I bring you good news. It will bring great joy for all the people. Today in the town of David a Savior has been born to you. He is the Messiah, the Lord. Here is how you will know I am telling you the truth. You will find a baby wrapped in strips of cloth and lying in a manger."

Suddenly a large group of angels from heaven also appeared. They were praising God. They said,

"May glory be given to God in the highest heaven! And may peace be given to those he is pleased with on earth!"

The angels left and went into heaven. Then the shepherds hurried off and found Mary and Joseph and the baby. The baby was lying in the manger. After the shepherds had seen him, they told everyone what the angel had said about this child. All who heard it were amazed.

SUPER ME

Jesus was the greatest hero who ever lived. He grew up to be the Savior of everyone in the world—including you! When you choose to believe in Jesus, he will erase all your sins and save a place for you in heaven. He will love you and watch over you for your whole life on earth. What could be better than that?

POWER SURGE

ULTIMATE SUPER HERO

"So the holy one that is born will be called the Son of God."
—Luke 1:35

WISE MEN

Matthew 2:1–12

Jesus was born in Bethlehem in Judea. This happened while Herod was king of Judea. After Jesus' birth, Wise Men from the east came to Jerusalem. They asked, "Where is the child who has been born to be king of the Jews? We saw his star when it rose. Now we have come to worship him."

When King Herod heard about it, he was very upset. So Herod called together all the chief priests of the people. He also called the teachers of the law. He asked them where the Messiah was going to be born. "In Bethlehem in Judea," they replied. "This is what the prophet has written."

Then Herod secretly called for the Wise Men. He found out from them exactly when the star had appeared.

He sent them to Bethlehem. He said, "Go and search carefully for the child. As soon as you find him, report it to me. Then I can go and worship him too."

After the Wise Men had listened to the king, they went on their way. The star they had seen when it rose went ahead of them.

It finally stopped over the place where the child was. When they saw the star, they were filled with joy. The Wise Men went to the house. There they saw the child with his mother Mary. They bowed down and worshiped him. Then they opened their treasures. They gave him gold, frankincense and myrrh. But God warned them in a dream not to go back to Herod. So they returned to their country on a different road.

SUPER ME

The Wise Men believed in Jesus and gave him gifts. Be as wise as these men. The wisest thing you can do in life is to believe Jesus and follow him.

POWER SURGE

GIVING G

"The Wise Men went to the house. There they saw the child with his mother Mary. They bowed down and worshiped him. Then they opened their treasures. They gave him gold, frankincense and myrrh."

—Matthew 2:11

SIMEON MEETS JESUS IN THE TEMPLE

Luke 2:22–35

Joseph and Mary took Jesus to Jerusalem. There they presented him to the Lord.

In Jerusalem there was a man named Simeon. He was a good and godly man. He was waiting for God's promise to Israel to come true. The Holy Spirit was with him. The Spirit had told Simeon that he would not die before he had seen the Lord's Messiah. The Spirit led him into the temple courtyard. Then Jesus' parents brought the child in. They came to do for him what the Law required.

Simeon took Jesus in his arms and praised God. He said,

"Lord, you are the King over all.
Now let me, your servant, go in peace.
That is what you promised.
My eyes have seen your salvation.
You have prepared it in the sight of all nations.
It is a light to be given to the Gentiles.
It will be the glory of your people Israel."

The child's father and mother were amazed at what was said about him. Then Simeon blessed them.

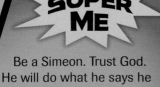

SUPER ME

Be a Simeon. Trust God. He will do what he says he will do. This is his promise. And he always keeps his promise.

POWER SURGE

PATIENT (P)

"The Spirit had told Simeon that he would not die before he had seen the Lord's Messiah."
—Luke 2:38

JESUS IS BAPTIZED

Mark 1:1–8; Matthew 3:13–17

JOHN THE BAPTIST

Long ago Isaiah the prophet wrote, "I will send my messenger ahead of you. He will prepare your way. A messenger is calling out in the desert, 'Prepare the way for the Lord. Make straight paths for him.'"

146

And so John the Baptist appeared in the desert. He preached that people should be baptized and turn away from their sins. Then God would forgive them. All the people from the countryside of Judea went out to him. All the people from Jerusalem went too. When they admitted they had sinned, John baptized them in the Jordan River.

John wore clothes made out of camel's hair. He had a leather belt around his waist. And he ate locusts and wild honey. Here is what John was preaching. "After me, there is someone coming who is more powerful than I am. I'm not good enough to bend down and untie his sandals. I baptize you with water. But he will baptize you with the Holy Spirit."

Jesus came from Galilee to the Jordan River. He wanted to be baptized by John. But John tried to stop him. So he told Jesus, "I need to be baptized by you. So why do you come to me?"

Jesus replied, "Let it be this way for now. It is right for us to do this. It carries out God's holy plan." Then John agreed.

As soon as Jesus was baptized, he came up out of the water. At that moment heaven was opened. Jesus saw the Spirit of God coming down on him like a dove. A voice from heaven said, "This is my Son, and I love him. I am very pleased with him."

SUPER ME

John the Baptist came before Jesus to get people ready for Jesus. He knew Jesus was the Savior of the world. He told people they needed to follow Jesus. You can be like John too. Tell your friends about Jesus.

POWER SURGE

BELIEVES ✚

"I baptize you with water, calling you to turn away from your sins. But after me, someone is coming who is more powerful than I am."

—Matthew 3:11

JESUS FEEDS
THE 5,000
Matthew 10:2–4; John 6:1–15

Here are the names of the 12 apostles. First there were Simon Peter and his brother Andrew. Then came James, son of Zebedee, and his brother John. Next were Philip and Bartholomew, and also Thomas and Matthew the tax collector. Two more were James, son of Alphaeus, and Thaddaeus. The last were Simon the Zealot and Judas Iscariot. Judas was the one who was later going to hand Jesus over to his enemies.

Jesus went up on a mountainside. There he sat down with his disciples. Jesus looked up and saw a large crowd coming toward him.

THE DISCIPLES

SIMON PETER

ANDREW

JAMES

JOHN

PHILIP

BARTHOLOMEW

THOMAS

MATTHEW

JAMES

THADDAEUS

SIMON

JUDAS

So he said to Philip, "Where can we buy bread for these people to eat?" He asked this only to test Philip. He already knew what he was going to do.

Philip answered him, "Suppose we were able to buy enough bread for each person to have just a bite. That would take more than half a year's pay!"

Another of his disciples spoke up. It was Andrew, Simon Peter's brother. He said, "Here is a boy with five small loaves of barley bread. He also has two small fish. But how far will that go in such a large crowd?"

Jesus said, "Have the people sit down." There was plenty of grass in that place, and they sat down. About 5,000 men were there. Then Jesus took the loaves and gave thanks. He handed out the bread to those who were seated. He gave them as much as they wanted. And he did the same with the fish.

When all of them had enough to eat, Jesus spoke to his disciples. "Gather the leftover pieces," he said. "Don't waste anything." So they gathered what was left over from the five barley loaves. They filled 12 baskets with the pieces left by those who had eaten.

The people saw the sign that Jesus did. Then they began to say, "This must be the Prophet who is supposed to come into the world."

SUPER ME

Wherever Jesus went, his twelve disciples went with him. They were eager to learn from him. You can learn about Jesus from the Bible and from other people. Are you like the disciple? Are you eager to learn about Jesus?

POWER SURGE

BELIEVES ✝

TRIES HARD T

"Blessed is anyone who does not give up their faith because of me."
—Matthew 11:6

JESUS HEALS

Matthew 8:5–13

When Jesus entered Capernaum, a Roman commander came to him. He asked Jesus for help. "Lord," he said, "my servant lies at home and can't move. He is suffering terribly."

Jesus said, "Shall I come and heal him?"

The commander replied, "Lord, I am not good enough to have you come into my house. But just say the word, and my servant will be healed. I myself am a man under authority. And I have soldiers who obey my orders. I tell this one, 'Go,' and he goes. I tell that one, 'Come,' and he comes. I say to my slave, 'Do this,' and he does it."

ROMAN COMMANDER

When Jesus heard this, he was amazed. He said to those following him, "What I'm about to tell you is true. In Israel I have not found anyone whose faith is so strong."

SUPER ME

Do you believe in Jesus? Do you believe he can do anything? Is your faith strong like the Roman commander's? If it isn't, pray and ask Jesus to give you more faith. He will do it.

Then Jesus said to the Roman commander, "Go! It will be done just as you believed it would." And his servant was healed at that moment.

POWER SURGE

BELIEVES †

"When Jesus heard this, he was amazed. He said to those following him, 'What I'm about to tell you is true. In Israel I have not found anyone whose faith is so strong.'"

—Matthew 8:10, 13

JESUS WALKS ON WATER

Matthew 14:22–33

PETER

Jesus made the disciples get into the boat. He had them go on ahead of him to the other side of the Sea of Galilee. He went up on a mountainside by himself to pray.

Later that night, he was there alone. The boat was already a long way from land. It was being pounded by the waves because the wind was blowing against it.

Shortly before dawn, Jesus went out to the disciples. He walked on the lake. They saw him walking on the lake and were terrified. "It's a ghost!" they said. And they cried out in fear.

Right away Jesus called out to them, "Be brave! It is I. Don't be afraid."

"Lord, is it you?" Peter asked. "If it is, tell me to come to you on the water."

"Come," Jesus said.

So Peter got out of the boat. He walked on the water toward Jesus. But when Peter saw the wind, he was afraid. He began to sink. He cried out, "Lord! Save me!"

Right away Jesus reached out his hand and caught him. "Your faith is so small!" he said. "Why did you doubt me?"

When they climbed into the boat, the wind died down. Then those in the boat worshiped Jesus. They said, "You really are the Son of God!"

SUPER ME

Don't be like Peter, but do. Believe in the power of the Lord to protect you. Ask Jesus to save you from your troubles and then let him do all the worrying for you.

POWER SURGE

BRAVE B

"Jesus called out to them, 'Be brave! It is I. Don't be afraid.'"

—Matthew 14:27

A HEALING TOUCH

Mark 5:21–34

A SICK WOMAN

Jesus went across the Sea of Galilee in a boat. There a large crowd gathered around him. A woman was there who had a sickness that made her bleed. It had lasted for 12 years. She had suffered a great deal, even though she had gone to many doctors. She had spent all the money she had. But she was getting worse, not better.

Then she heard about Jesus. She came up behind him in the crowd and touched his clothes. She thought, "I just need to touch his clothes. Then I will be healed." Right away her bleeding stopped. She felt in her body that her suffering was over.

At once Jesus knew that power had gone out from him. He turned around in the crowd. He asked, "Who touched my clothes?"

"You see the people," his disciples answered. "They are crowding against you. And you still ask, 'Who touched me?'"

But Jesus kept looking around. He wanted to see who had touched him. Then the woman came and fell at his feet. She knew what had happened to her. She was shaking with fear. But she told him the whole truth.

He said to her, "Dear woman, your faith has healed you. Go in peace. You are free from your suffering."

SUPER ME

When you need something from God, don't wait for him to act. Go to him and ask for his help. He loves you enough and will help you whenever you need him.

POWER SURGE

BELIEVES ✝

"Don't be afraid. Just believe."
—Mark 5:36

ZACCHAEUS
CLIMBS A TREE
Luke 19:1–10

Jesus entered Jericho. A man named Zacchaeus lived there. He was a chief tax collector and was very rich. Zacchaeus wanted to see who Jesus was. But he was a short man. He could not see Jesus because of the crowd. So he ran ahead and climbed a sycamore-fig tree. He wanted to see Jesus, who was coming that way.

Jesus reached the spot where Zacchaeus was. He looked up and said, "Zacchaeus, come down at once. I must stay at your house today." So Zacchaeus came down at once and welcomed him gladly.

All the people saw this. They began to whisper among themselves. They said, "Jesus has gone to be the guest of a sinner."

But Zacchaeus stood up. He said, "Look, Lord! Here and now I give half of what I own to those who are poor. And if I have cheated anybody out of anything, I will pay it back. I will pay back four times the amount I took."

Jesus said to Zacchaeus, "Today salvation has come to your house. The Son of Man came to look for the lost and save them."

SUPER ME

Be a Zacchaeus. Don't be afraid of what others might think. Be sure you search for Jesus and follow his truths. If it makes you look a little foolish, follow Jesus with all your heart, just like Zacchaeus.

POWER SURGE

GIVING G

"But Zacchaeus stood up. He said, "Look, Lord! Here and now I give half of what I own to those who are poor. And if I have cheated anybody out of anything, I will pay it back. I will pay back four times the amount I took.'"

—Luke 19:8

THE GREAT GIFT

Luke 20:1; 21:1–4

WIDOW WITH TWO COINS

One day Jesus was teaching the people in the temple courtyard. He was announcing the good news to them.

As Jesus looked up, he saw rich people putting their gifts into the temple offering boxes. He also saw a poor widow put in two very small copper coins.

"What I'm about to tell you is true," Jesus said. "That poor widow has put in more than all the others. All these other people gave a lot because they are rich. But even though she is poor, she put in everything. She had nothing left to live on."

What do you have to give to God? You can have many gifts to give or only a few. What matters to God is that you give it, trusting him to care for you. Be like this widow! Give your gifts to God because you love him, not because others will be impressed with your gift.

⚡POWER SURGE

GIVING Ⓖ

"'What I'm about to tell you is true,' Jesus said. 'That poor widow has put in more than all the others … even though she is poor, she put in everything.'"

—Luke 21:3–4

179

JESUS DIES FOR OUR SINS

Luke 22

The Feast of Unleavened Bread, called the Passover, was near. Peter and John prepared the Passover meal. When the hour came, Jesus and his apostles took their places at the table. He said to them, "I have really looked forward to eating this Passover meal with you. I tell you, I will not eat the Passover meal again until it is celebrated in God's kingdom."

Jesus took bread. He gave thanks and broke it. He handed it to them and said, "This is my body. It is given for you. Every time you eat it, do this in memory of me." In the same way, after the supper he took the cup. He said, "This cup is the new covenant in my blood. It is poured out for you."

Jesus went to the Mount of Olives. There he got down on his knees and prayed. An angel from heaven appeared to Jesus and gave him strength.

A crowd came up. The man named Judas was leading them. The men arrested Jesus and led him away. The soldiers brought them to the place called the Skull. There they nailed Jesus to the cross.

It was now about noon. Darkness covered the whole land until three o'clock. Jesus called out in a loud voice, "Father, into your hands I commit my life." After he said this, he took his last breath.

SUPER ME

Jesus loved us so much that he gave his life for us on this cross. Because of his sacrifice, we can one day join him in heaven. What an incredible act of selflessness! Is there something selfless you can do to show others you love them? It doesn't have to be a big act like Jesus'--even the smallest gestures can show you care.

POWER SURGE

ULTIMATE SUPER HERO

"God so loved the world that he gave his one and only Son. Anyone who believes in him will not die but will have eternal life."

—John 3:16

183

JESUS HAS RISEN!

John 19:41–42; 20:1–18

MARY MAGDALENE

At the place where Jesus was crucified, there was a garden. A new tomb was there. No one had ever been put in it before. So they placed Jesus there.

Early on the first day of the week, Mary Magdalene went to the tomb. She saw that the stone had been moved away from the entrance. So she ran to Simon Peter and another disciple. She said, "They have taken the Lord out of the tomb! We don't know where they have put him!"

So Peter and the other disciple started out for the tomb. Both of them were running. The other disciple ran faster than Peter. He reached the tomb first. He bent over and looked in at the strips of linen lying there. Then Simon Peter came along behind him. He also saw the funeral cloth that had been wrapped around Jesus' head. They still did not understand from Scripture that Jesus had to rise from the dead. Then the disciples went back to where they were staying.

But Mary stood outside the tomb crying. As she cried, she bent over to look into the tomb. She saw two angels dressed in white. They were seated where Jesus' body had been.

They asked her, "Woman, why are you crying?"

"They have taken my Lord away," she said. "I don't know where they have put him."

Then she turned around and saw Jesus standing there. But she didn't realize that it was Jesus.

He asked her, "Woman, why are you crying? Who are you looking for?"

She thought he was the gardener. So she said, "Sir, did you carry him away? Tell me where you put him. Then I will go and get him."

Jesus said to her, "Mary."

She turned toward him. Then she cried out in the Aramaic language, "Rabboni!" Rabboni means Teacher.

Jesus said, "Go to those who believe in me. Tell them, 'I am ascending to my Father and your Father, to my God and your God.'"

187

Mary Magdalene went to the disciples with the news. She said, "I have seen the Lord!" And she told them that he had said these things to her.

SUPER ME

Mary's love for Jesus made her want to do whatever she could to help him. How can you be like Mary? Could you help someone in need? Could you tell someone about Jesus' love? There are many ways you can be like Mary. Be on the lookout. You'll find a way!

POWER SURGE

BELIEVES ✝

"These are written so that you may believe that Jesus is the Messiah, the Son of God. If you believe this, you will have life because you belong to him."
—John 20:31

SHARING THE NEWS ABOUT JESUS

Acts 3:1–9; 4:1–26

JOHN

One day Peter and John were going up to the temple. A man unable to walk was being carried to the temple gate. Peter looked straight at him, and so did John. Peter said, "In the name of Jesus Christ of Nazareth, get up and walk."

At once the man's feet and ankles became strong. He jumped to his feet and began to walk.

The priests, the captain of the temple guard, and the Sadducees came up to the apostles. They were very upset by what the apostles were teaching the people.

So the temple authorities arrested Peter and John. It was already evening, so they put them in prison until the next day. But many who heard the message believed. The number of men who believed grew to about 5,000.

The next day the rulers, the elders and the teachers of the law met in Jerusalem. They had Peter and John brought to them.

Peter was filled with the Holy Spirit. He said to them, "Rulers and elders of the people! Are you asking us to explain our actions today? Do you want to know why we were kind to a man who couldn't walk? Are you asking how he was healed? It is through Jesus' name that this man stands healed in front of you."

The leaders saw how bold Peter and John were. They realized that these men had been with Jesus. The leaders could see the man who had been healed. He was standing there with them. So there was nothing they could say. They ordered Peter and John to leave. They commanded them not to speak or teach at all in Jesus' name.

But Peter and John replied, "Which is right from God's point of view? Should we listen to you? Or should we listen to God? You be the judges! There's nothing else we can do. We have to speak about the things we've seen and heard."

The leaders warned them again. Then they let them go. They couldn't decide how to punish Peter and John. They knew that all the people were praising God for what had happened.

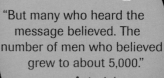

SUPER ME

John was in danger. These officials could punish him. But he only knew one thing. He had to speak about Jesus. Be like John. You may think you don't have the courage, but you do. Your courage comes from the same place John got his—from Jesus.

POWER SURGE

BELIEVES ✝

TELLS OTHERS 🗣

"But many who heard the message believed. The number of men who believed grew to about 5,000."
—Acts 4:4

STEPHEN IS ARRESTED

Acts 6:8–8:3

Stephen was full of God's grace and power. He did great wonders and signs among the people. But members of the group called the Synagogue of the Freedmen began to oppose him. They all began to argue with Stephen. But he was too wise for them. That's because the Holy Spirit gave Stephen wisdom whenever he spoke.

Then in secret they talked some men into lying about Stephen. They said, "We heard Stephen speak evil things against Moses and against God." So the people were stirred up. The elders and the teachers of the law were stirred up too.

B

STEPHEN

They arrested Stephen. They found witnesses who were willing to tell lies. These liars said, "This fellow never stops speaking against this holy place. He also speaks against the law. We have heard him say that this Jesus of Nazareth will destroy this place. He says Jesus will change the practices that Moses handed down to us."

Then the high priest questioned Stephen. "Is what these people are saying true?" he asked.

"Brothers and fathers, listen to me!" Stephen replied. "You stubborn people! You won't obey! You won't listen! You always oppose the Holy Spirit!"

When the members of the Sanhedrin heard this, they became very angry. They were so angry they ground their teeth at Stephen. But he was full of the Holy Spirit. He looked up to heaven and saw God's glory. He saw Jesus standing at God's right hand. "Look!" he said. "I see heaven open. The Son of Man is standing at God's right hand."

When the Sanhedrin heard this, they covered their ears. They yelled at the top of their voices. They all rushed at him. They dragged him out of the city. They began to throw stones at him to kill him.

While the members of the Sanhedrin were throwing stones at Stephen, he prayed. "Lord Jesus, receive my spirit," he said. Then he fell on his knees. He cried out, "Lord! Don't hold this sin against them!" When he had said this, he died.

SUPER ME

You will probably never be killed for following Jesus. But you may be mocked or laughed at. Be a Stephen. Be strong and brave in the face of those who make fun of you. Jesus will give you strength to stand your ground, to stand up for what you believe in. You just have to ask and trust him.

POWER SURGE

STRONG

"Stephen was full of God's grace and power."

—Acts 6:8

PHILIP AND THE ETHIOPIAN

Acts 8:26–40

An angel of the Lord spoke to Philip. "Go south to the desert road," he said. "It's the road that goes down from Jerusalem to Gaza." So Philip started out. On his way he met an Ethiopian official. This official had gone to Jerusalem to worship.

On his way home he was sitting in his chariot. He was reading the Book of Isaiah the prophet. The Holy Spirit told Philip, "Go to that chariot. Stay near it."

So Philip ran up to the chariot. He heard the man reading Isaiah the prophet. "Do you understand what you're reading?" Philip asked.

PHILIP

"How can I?" he said. "I need someone to explain it to me." So he invited Philip to come up and sit with him.

Here is the part of Scripture the official was reading. It says,

"He was led like a sheep to be killed.
Just as lambs are silent while their wool is
being cut off,
he did not open his mouth.
When he was treated badly,
he was refused a fair trial.
Who can say anything about his children?
His life was cut off from the earth."

The official said to Philip, "Tell me, please. Who is the prophet talking about? Himself, or someone else?" Then Philip began with that same part of Scripture. He told him the good news about Jesus.

As they traveled along the road, they came to some water.
The official said, "Look! Here is water! What can stop me
from being baptized?" He gave orders to stop the chariot.
Then both Philip and the official went down into the water.
Philip baptized him. The official went on his way full of joy.

SUPER ME

Philip didn't keep the good news about Jesus to himself. He told others so that they could believe too. Be a Philip. Tell others about Jesus and his love.

POWER SURGE

BELIEVES †

TELLS OTHERS 🗣

"Philip announced the good news of God's kingdom and the name of Jesus Christ. So men and women believed and were baptized."

—Acts 8:12

BLINDED BY THE LIGHT

Acts 9:1–31

Saul continued to oppose the Lord's followers. He said they would be put to death. He wanted to find men and women who belonged to the Way of Jesus. On his journey, Saul approached Damascus.

Suddenly a light from heaven flashed around him. He fell to the ground. He heard a voice speak to him, "Saul! Saul! Why are you opposing me?"

"Who are you, Lord?" Saul asked.

"I am Jesus," he replied. "I am the one you are opposing. Now get up and go into the city. There you will be told what you must do."

The men traveling with Saul had heard the sound. But they didn't see anyone. Saul got up from the ground. He opened his eyes, but he couldn't see. So they led him by the hand into Damascus. For three days he was blind.

In Damascus there was a believer named Ananias. The Lord called out to him in a vision. "Ananias!" he said.

"Yes, Lord," he answered.

The Lord told him, "Go to the house of Judas on Straight Street. Ask for a man from Tarsus named Saul and place hands on him."

"Lord," Ananias answered, "I've heard many reports about this man. They say he has done great harm to your holy people in Jerusalem."

But the Lord said to Ananias, "Go! I have chosen this man to work for me. He will announce my name to the Gentiles and to their kings. He will also announce my name to the people of Israel."

Then Ananias went to the house and entered it. He placed his hands on Saul. "Brother Saul," he said, "you saw the Lord Jesus. He has sent me so that you will be able to see again. You will be filled with the Holy Spirit." Right away something like scales fell from Saul's eyes. And he could see again. He got up and was baptized.

Saul spent several days with the believers in Damascus. Right away he began to preach in the synagogues. He taught that Jesus is the Son of God. All who heard him were amazed. Saul proved to them that Jesus is the Messiah.

SUPER ME

Saul hated Christians. You don't want to be like that. But Saul immediately followed Jesus when he discovered the truth. Whenever you learn something new and exciting about God, be like Saul. Follow God and obey him wherever you are.

POWER SURGE

TELLS OTHERS

"So Saul stayed with the believers. He moved about freely in Jerusalem. He spoke boldly in the Lord's name."
—Acts 9:28

THE JAILER

Acts 13:9, 16

Saul was also known as Paul. He was filled with the Holy Spirit. Paul and his companions traveled all through the area of Phrygia and Galatia. [Some slave owners] grabbed Paul and Silas. They brought them to the judges. The judges ordered that Paul and Silas be beaten with rods. Then they were thrown into prison. The jailer was commanded to guard them carefully. When he received these orders, he put Paul and Silas deep inside the prison. He fastened their feet so they couldn't get away.

About midnight Paul and Silas were praying. They were also singing hymns to God. The other prisoners were listening to them. Suddenly there was a powerful earthquake. It shook the prison from top to bottom.

All at once the prison doors flew open. Everyone's chains came loose. The jailer woke up. He saw that the prison doors were open. He pulled out his sword and was going to kill himself. He thought the prisoners had escaped. "Don't harm yourself!" Paul shouted. "We are all here!"

The jailer called out for some lights. He rushed in, shaking with fear. He fell down in front of Paul and Silas. Then he brought them out. He asked, "Sirs, what must I do to be saved?"

They replied, "Believe in the Lord Jesus. Then you and everyone living in your house will be saved." They spoke the word of the Lord to him.

At that hour of the night, the jailer took Paul and Silas and washed their wounds. Right away he and everyone who lived with him were baptized. The jailer brought them into his house. He set a meal in front of them. He and everyone who lived with him were filled with joy. They had become believers in God.

SUPER ME

As soon as the jailer knew what happened, he asked Paul and Silas what he needed to do to be saved. He didn't want to waste one minute. You can be like the jailer too. Don't waste your time. Decide today that you will follow Jesus. Then be like the jailer, and do it!

POWER SURGE

BELIEVES ✝

"The jailer … and everyone who lived with him were filled with joy. They had become believers in God."
—Acts 16:34

YOU!

All the heroes of the Bible are examples of what you can be for Jesus.

Joshua was scared, but God helped him be brave.

Deborah was a woman, but she led an army.

David was little, but God used him to fight a huge giant.

Isaiah felt full of sin, but God told him he would use him anyway.

God doesn't want you to think that you have to be just like these people. He wants you to be you.

The heroes of the Bible were plain, ordinary people. Many of them were not as obedient as they should have been. Many of them were scared. Many of them were weak. Maybe you are all those things too.

But one thing all of the heroes had in common is that they were willing to let God use them.

That's all Jesus asks of you too. Just be willing.
Don't ever start to think you're too young.

Or not smart enough.

Or not strong enough.

Or not brave enough.

Jesus only asks you to be willing.

He'll give you the smarts and the strength and the bravery to do as he asks.

SUPER ME

This is the end of the storybook Bible. But don't let it be the end of the super heroes. In this book you've read other heroes' code of honor. What is your code of honor? God will help you be a super hero for him!

POWER SURGE

"I can do all this by the power of Christ. He gives me strength."

—Philippians 4:13